A Look at Egypt

by Helen Frost

Consulting Editor: Gail Saunders-Smith, Ph.D.

Consultant: Cemal Kafadar, Ph.D., Professor
History of the Middle East
Center for Middle East Studies
Harvard University

Pebble Books

an imprint of Capstone Press
Mankato, Minnesota

Pebble Books are published by Capstone Press
151 Good Counsel Drive, P.O. Box 669, Mankato, Minnesota 56002
http://www.capstone-press.com

1 2 3 4 5 6 07 06 05 04 03 02

Library of Congress Cataloging-in-Publication Data
Frost, Helen, 1949–
    A look at Egypt / by Helen Frost.
      p. cm.—(Our world)
      Summary: Simple text and photographs introduce the land, people,
animals, transportation, and monuments of Egypt.
      Includes bibliographical references and index.
      ISBN 0-7368-1429-9 (hardcover)
      ISBN 0-7368-9390-3 (paperback)
      1. Egypt—Juvenile literature. [1. Egypt.] I. Title. II. Series.
DT49 .F76   2003
962—dc21   2001007770

CURR

Note to Parents and Teachers

The Our World series supports national social studies standards
related to culture. This book describes and illustrates the land,
animals, and people of Egypt. The images support early readers
in understanding the text. The repetition of words and phrases
helps early readers learn new words. This book also introduces
early readers to subject-specific vocabulary words, which are
defined in the Words to Know section. Early readers may need
assistance to read some words and to use the Table of Contents,
Words to Know, Read More, Internet Sites, and Index/Word List
sections of the book.

Table of Contents

★
Cairo

Egypt

N
W ← → E
S

Egypt is a country
in northeast Africa.
The capital of Egypt
is Cairo. Cairo is one
of the largest cities
in the world.

Egypt's flag

Most of Egypt is desert. The desert is very hot during the day. The desert is very cold at night.

egret

sand cat

8

Egrets live by
the Nile River in Egypt.
Sand cats live
in Egypt's deserts.

More than 68 million
people live in Egypt.
Most people live near
the Nile River. Egyptians
speak and write
the Arabic language.

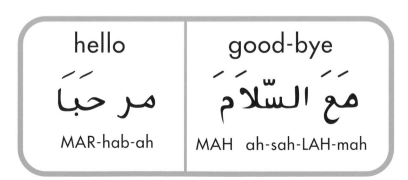

hello	good-bye
مـرحبًا	مَعَ السّلاَمَ
MAR-hab-ah	MAH ah-sah-LAH-mah

Egyptian farmer growing dates

Farmers in Egypt grow dates, corn, and cotton to earn money. Workers make clothing, rubber, and cement.

Egypt's money is counted in Egyptian pounds.

Many people in Egypt travel by car, bus, and airplane. They also travel by train and boat. People ride camels in Egypt's deserts.

Ancient Egyptian art tells stories through pictures. Some art shows people working. Other art shows kings, queens, and gods.

Pyramids are big stone monuments shaped like triangles. Egyptians built the pyramids a long time ago.

The Great Sphinx is
a huge statue in Egypt.
The Great Sphinx has
the head of a human.
It has the body of a lion.

Words to Know

Africa—one of the seven continents of the world

Arabic—a written and spoken language; Arabic is used in Egypt and some other countries in the Middle East.

capital—the city in a country where the government is based

cement—a gray powder that is used to make buildings; cement becomes hard when it is mixed with water and left to dry.

date—a kind of fruit; Egypt grows the most dates in the world.

egret—a tall bird with white feathers

Nile River—the longest river in the world; the Nile is 3,473 miles (5,589 kilometers) long.

rubber—a strong, elastic substance used to make items such as tires, balls, and boots

sand cat—a small wild cat that lives in the desert

Read More

Deady, Kathleen W. *Egypt.* Countries of the World. Mankato, Minn.: Bridgestone Books, 2001.

Frank, Nicole, and Susan L. Wilson. *Welcome to Egypt.* Welcome to My Country. Milwaukee: Gareth Stevens, 2000.

Landau, Elaine. *Egypt.* A True Book. New York: Children's Press, 2000.

Ryan, Patrick. *Egypt.* Faces and Places. Chanhassen, Minn.: Child's World, 1999.

Internet Sites

Ancient Egypt
http://tqjunior.thinkquest.org/4368/?tqskip=1

Egypt Quiz
http://www.enchantedlearning.com/
classroom/quiz/egypt.shtml

Wild Egypt: An Online Safari
http://touregypt.net/wildegypt

Index/Word List

Word Count: 179
Early-Intervention Level: 17

Editorial Credits
Mari C. Schuh, editor; Kia Adams, series designer; Jennifer Schonborn and Patrick D. Dentinger, book designers; Alta Schaffer, photo researcher

Photo Credits
Digital Stock, 1, 6
International Stock/Michael Lichter, cover; Tom & Michele Grimm, 16; Hilary Wilkes, 20
John Elk III, 10, 14, 18
One Mile Up, Inc., 5
Trip/M. Jellife, 12
Visuals Unlimited/G.L.E., 8 (top); Ken Lucas, 8 (bottom)

DATE DUE